How Will I Grow?

Mick Manning
and Brita Granström

W

FRANKLIN WATTS
LONDON·SYDNEY

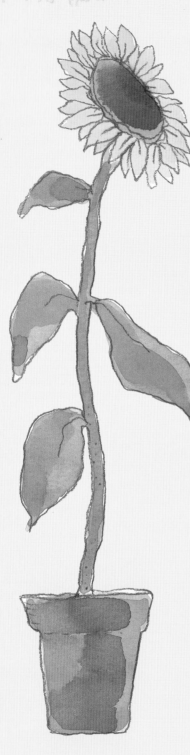

Rock on, Charlotte!

This edition 2004
First published in 2002 by Franklin Watts,
96 Leonard Street, London EC2A 4XD

Franklin Watts Australia
45-51 Huntley Street, Alexandria, NSW 2015

Text and illustrations © 2002 Mick Manning
and Brita Granström

The illustrations in this book have
been drawn by Brita
Find out more about Mick and Brita
on www.mickandbrita.com

Series editor: Rachel Cooke
Art director: Jonathan Hair

Printed in Hong Kong, China
A CIP catalogue record is available from
the British Library.
Dewey Classification 612
ISBN 0 7496 5663 8

Contents

How did I grow to be this big?

You have been growing right from the moment you were made by your mum and dad. For 9 months you grew inside your mum's tummy.

Then once you were born you really started to grow . . . You doubled your weight in the first few weeks!

All parts of you started to develop at an amazing speed. Your bones got longer and stronger. And your skin and muscles grew like mad to support the bones.

Your bones have soft cartilage at the ends. As this grows, it hardens and makes the bones longer and stronger.

And your body is still growing: your skin, muscles, bones, heart and lungs . . .

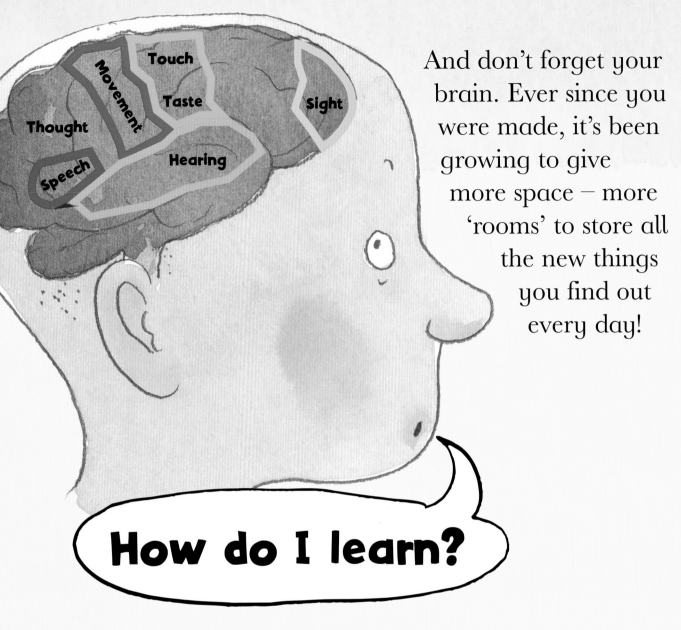

And don't forget your brain. Ever since you were made, it's been growing to give more space – more 'rooms' to store all the new things you find out every day!

How do I learn?

You learn from using all your senses – from listening, looking, feeling, tasting and smelling.

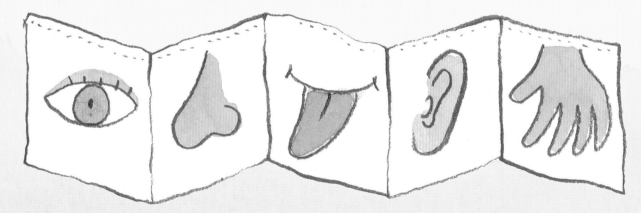

You began learning inside your mum's tummy. By the time you were born, you could already recognise her voice.

After that you learned all the time: playing with your toys, tasting your food, even by bouncing on your dad's knee or being tickled by granny!

So I learned to walk?

Your bones and muscles grew and you made them stronger by crawling and climbing, and practising standing. At about the age of 1, you were strong enough to start walking. You fell over a bit to begin with . . . but practice makes perfect!

And when did I talk?

You made lots of noises even when you were very tiny. You learned by listening and copying. At about 1 year old, you were saying whole words and around 2 you could put sentences together. Now you and your friends can chatter away like magpies!

Some children grow up speaking two languages if their mum and dad are from different countries. They grow up hearing two languages so speaking both comes naturally.

Is it easy to learn?

Of course it is. All children are very brainy. They learn and remember much quicker than grown-ups can.

As well as learning to read and count, your brain and body work together to learn balance and co-ordination, so you can catch balls, ride bikes and swim.

Growing brains work best when lessons are mixed with lots of exercise, like running, climbing and jumping. So playtime helps you learn more!

And when did my teeth grow?

Your teeth were already under your gums when you were born. After 6 months, you began teething. One or two at a time, your teeth pushed out of your gums. You had started to eat solid food then as well so you could grow even faster. By the time you were 2, you had 20 teeth.

You need to brush your teeth at least twice a day to keep them clean and healthy. If your adult teeth drop out, you won't grow any new ones!

So why are my teeth dropping out?

Your first teeth are your milk teeth. Between about ages 6 and 8, they are replaced by 32 adult ones. These are bigger and stronger – and should last your whole life, so long as you look after them!

How a tooth is made

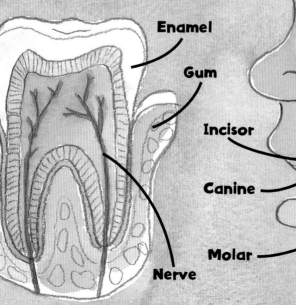

- Enamel
- Gum
- Incisor
- Canine
- Molar
- Nerve
- Adult teeth

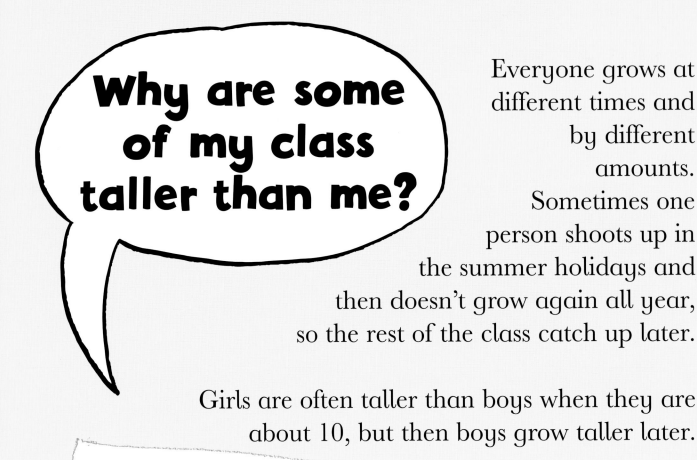

Why are some of my class taller than me?

Everyone grows at different times and by different amounts. Sometimes one person shoots up in the summer holidays and then doesn't grow again all year, so the rest of the class catch up later.

Girls are often taller than boys when they are about 10, but then boys grow taller later.

It's hard to say exactly. If there are lots of tall people in your family, then you'll probably be tall too.

Men usually grow taller than women. But it doesn't matter how tall or small you are when you're older, so long as you are well and happy. People still love you just the same.

Do I have to eat my greens?

If you want to grow up strong and healthy, then yes, you have to eat all sorts of food – including green vegetables.

Pasta, green salad and an apple make a healthy meal.

Chips are yum! But eat other things with them. Always drink lots of water.

Soup and a roll with yogurt to follow is a good light lunch.

You need a mix of food for your body to work properly, but you shouldn't eat too much of some things. Eating lots of sweets and other sugary food is bad for you.

Different foods are good for you in different ways, which is why you need a mixture.

Food that fills you up, like pasta and potatoes, gives you energy.

Vegetables have lots of fibre and vitamins to keep you healthy.

Meat, cheese and eggs help you grow and your muscles develop.

You need fat, like butter and oil, and a little sugar, too – which includes chocolate!

Rabbits know what's good for them!

Pizza's always good. Cucumber and orange juice add some extra goodness.

Sausages, potatoes and green spinach is a good mixture to help you grow up healthy.

When am I a teenager?

You'll be a teenager when you reach your 'teens' – on your thir*teen*th birthday. You'll have carried on growing and learning all the time. Your body will have started changing in different ways, too, getting ready to be able to make babies.

GIRLS

Sweat glands under the arms grow bigger.

Some girls get spots!

Breasts develop.

Periods begin (see page 21).

Hips broaden.

More hair grows under the arms and between the legs.

We call the way your body changes at this time puberty. Puberty happens to people at different times. Girls tend to go through puberty before boys.

So how will my body change?

During puberty, girls' and boys' bodies make chemicals called hormones. There are male and female hormones which make girls and boys change in different ways. Some changes are the same – both boys and girls grow a lot taller.

BOYS

Chest and shoulders broaden.

Hair grows under arms. Chest may get hairy too.

Penis and testicles grow larger. Hair grows around them.

Some boys get spots!

Hair grows on face. Shaving begins!

Sweat glands grow bigger under arms and on feet!

Will my voice change?

Girls' voices get a bit deeper as they grow older. But boys' voices change much more. Their vocal chords grow longer and their voices 'break'. They sound funny for a time.

*!

This and other changes in boys' bodies are triggered by male hormones, which are made in the testicles. The testicles also begin producing millions of sperm ready to make a baby.

Sperm tube

Penis

Testicle

Testicle

Scrotum

**!

To make a baby, sperm from the male must connect with a female egg cell (see opposite). To do this, men and women make love and have a special cuddle called sex.

What are periods?

Changes in girls' bodies during puberty are triggered by female hormones. These are made in the ovaries. The ovaries also contain thousands of egg cells.

Periods are part of these body changes. Once a month, an egg cell moves from one of the ovaries to the womb. If the girl does not get pregnant, the womb lining breaks down and, with the egg, passes out of the vagina. This causes bleeding.

Womb

Ovary

Ovary

Vagina

Girls use sanitary towels (STs) to stop the blood messing up their knickers. Later, instead of STs, they may use tampons which they insert inside the vagina.

What will puberty feel like?

Well, you may find you sweat more and get spots for a while. You'll probably need to wash a bit more carefully and change your socks more often. You might also find you feel more upset and moody.

Your body is changing so much and you are growing so fast that, for a while, it makes too many of the chemicals that help you feel happy or sad and this makes your moods change a lot.

And, of course, you'll start to like girls or boys in a different way . . . And that might make you feel very happy or very sad sometimes!

Will I make new friends?

Yes, you'll make new friends all through your life. They'll be people you share things in common with – maybe you'll laugh at the same things or have the same interests. You'll make friends at clubs or maybe through sport or your hobbies.

Some people you'll like straight away and some people might take a while to get to know.

What's love?

There are lots of different sorts of love. There's the loving feeling you have for your family and your home. As you get older, you might start to feel love for other boys or girls your own age. Sometimes this can become a very strong feeling and you'll want to be with them lots and lots.

Sometimes you can fall in love with a pop or film star. It feels just like the real thing at the time and you may have sleepless nights and dreamy days thinking about your idol! But it is probably just a crush and won't last long.

You stop growing taller sometime in your twenties, although you'll carry on maturing and changing in lots of other ways.

You'll leave school sometime in your late teens and maybe go to college or get a job. You may leave home about then too. But you don't have to! Some people like to live with their family a lot longer. Eventually, you may start a family of your own.

Whatever you decide your family will aways love you. And wherever you go and whatever you do . . .

You'll always be YOU!

HOW YOU WILL GROW (BOY)

Dad

Adult

Teenager

Baby

Toddler

School age

Nearly 10

30

Nearly 10

School age

Toddler

Baby

You're going to grow . . . and grow . . .

Teenager

Adult

Mum

31

Useful words

Cartilage is the soft, bendy substance that joins our muscles to our bones.

Co-ordination is the way we can move different parts of our bodies in the right way at the same time.

Fibre is the rough stuff in food which helps it pass through our bodies.

The **heart** pumps blood around our bodies. It is in our chests.

Hormones are chemicals in our bodies which make them change and grow.

Lungs are where we breathe air into and out of our bodies.

Maturing describes the way things change as they get older.

Muscles are what we use to make our bodies move.

Ovaries are the part inside women's bodies which hold the egg cells.

The **penis** hangs between a man's legs. He pees through it and, after puberty, sperm passes through it.

Periods are the monthly bleeding that women have from the womb once they reach puberty.

Pregnant describes a woman who is going to have a baby.

Puberty describes the changes people go through from about age 10 as their bodies prepare for making babies.

The **scrotum** contains a man's testicles.

Sweat glands grow under our skin and make sweat when we get hot.

Teething describes when babies' teeth are coming through their gums.

Testicles are the part of men's bodies where sperm is made.

The **vagina** is an opening in a woman's body between her legs which connects to her womb.

Vocal chords are flaps inside your throat which vibrate when you speak.

The **womb** is the part of a woman's body where new babies grow.

Index